This is how the medication works.

words by mobee.
music arrangements and catering by Justin .

Contents

this is how the medication works 9
i would buy you an orange cat 10
we talk loudly about revolution 11
coma in the hospital, coma in the rain 12
i had a crush on Daria and Jane 13
we make our first child and i throw it in the river 14
i'd rather be Anthony Bourdain than God 15
she used to chain me at her feet 16
i play death in my front yard 17
if you aren't too beautiful today 18
the muralist is a noted womanizer & gives crabs 19
i do not think the libs are coming 20
it's Wednesday morning 21
the hole in my mouth got wider 22
we were too many kids to be loved like kids 23
the moment i smelled all those other drunks 24
after my dad clicked his gun 25
we ripped a mailman to shreds 26
we are the things that stand between the birds 27
Lou Reed was a better poet than Keats 28
i don't want to go towards the light 29
if you hold me too close to the nervous system 30
you'd prefer to die but you are a small child 31
i am asked to tacitly scroll 32
the wolf at the door 33
i don't trust anyone who stiffs servers 34
come wet, i am hellishly drunk 35
anyone who loves me or my poems 36
you built a dumb house 37
we like to drown, Mae 38
i used to make mix cds for girls 39
everywhere in this hospital i am dying again 40
you said, "let's just have the baby" 41
we reach out with the entirety of our pain 42

i don't have anything left to feed the wolves 43
i carry a jar of your tiny flame 44
you're scared of a pussy 45
the cat is in my lap 46
it yelped & flew over the fence 47
there is a faint green that comes off of me 48
somewhere a lighthouse falls over 49
so i think we should wear the wolf masks to church 50
you do not know who the little crow asked me to be 51
don't drop your joy on a man 52
all those other drunks were wrong, not me 53
they will cut a little thing out of you 54
if anarchists have a dress code 55
i'm sick and i recognize i have no history 56
i was way too little to be your father 57
you are afraid now i'm gone 58
a mosquito lives in your rib cage 59
the moment i fingered the russian perfume salesperson 60
we take a metro to the local grocery 61
i plant seventeen communists in my garden 62
the workers have taken the South Carolina penitentiary 63
i had a nervous breakdown when i was 29 years old 64
j'adore your little cat 65
i barely slept on my grandmother's floor 66
i'm sorry i got drunk and ghosted your birthday party 67
i'm writing this poem for a book 68
mae, they don't understand how bored 69
i kissed eight girls on my last day in town 70
here's the perfect love poem 71
there are ten stray cats in my neighborhood 72
i know a system that killed my friend 73
i'm not worried if god knows i'm gay 74
today i woke up 75
i hope when they draw the blinds on you 76
we're uncommon fireflies 77
how do i tell the crow that i don't know 78
i will give you the secret to a good fuck 79
i don't drink to get anything out of it 80
the only reason we have mental hospitals 81

it comes every so often at night 82
my dad survived catapulting his head through a house 83
when i found your nothing 84
the bowl is cashed 85
they took my grandmother away with half her intestines 86
jesus died for my pedophilic bloodline 87
i could not trust my body 88
the thing i love about bars 89
this is how we move our bodies so close together 90
i am this pigeon trapped in the station 91
we like to build houses on other people's heads 92
i love the way you love horror movies 93
it is right there and you are not aware of it 94
it was such a brutal night, i did not find you 95
it is here in the mailman's suicide note 96
i am in love with no men, only cats 97
there is a nasty cut on my neck, mae 98
i fell with a woman mighty enough to own the spiders 99
at 16 i was given the option 100
i was supposed to be a priest 101
the way you kicked off your shoes, mae 102
mae, i'm the space between the loves 103
i have not emptied a bottle as strong 104
nothing hurts enough 105
don't hesitate to bleed out next to me 106
i read a very bad poem 107
i want to be well but 108
if you like this poem, well 109
the universe isn't a place, it is in mae 110
you ask me to narc on my friends 111
it sat hard on my chest at 5 years old 112
the moment the panic attack hits, i know 113
there is cellophane over the neighbors' flowers 114
you are too manic to kill the pixie 115
o 116
i of the moths i kill 117
if you stand between two planets 118
we had six-month old burrito wrappers under our asses 119
i come awake under the robins 120

please bring back my childhood cat 121
some mornings a little piece of dream comes with me 122
he lived under her legs at the local bar 123
if the darkest thing you can think of 124
we chased the tech bro 125
how many licks does it take 126
do not love so more 127
do not be a drug addict, mae 128
when you hold the little grey cat 129
war criminals don't just bomb 130
(plead insanity 131
i will start sending you letters 132
i used to shatter cds 133
i would open my legs 134
it is not a kind world, mae 135
there are two of me 136

to Kelsey

*this is how
the medication works.*

we'll be happy and
i'll be tired sometimes.

i'll grow old and draw
a lot of pretty pictures.

you'll be next to me and you'll have a
               great Understandin g
               of plants and death

i will love you as much as i can.

i would buy you
    an orange cat
       though you shouldn't buy cats

they should just be at your door
when you're near dead
    or closer.

Do you know i forgive you
before the cats and coroners come?

we talk loudly about revolution, so loud that the bartender closes the windows and sets her VPN to Sweden
i drink seven gin tonics & plot 46 ways 17 involve dead Russian authors. 22 are a form of fraud in 121 countries
six involve loving you, one involves no love at all.

coma in the hospital, coma in the rain
coma in the falling dreamers on xanax & wellbutrin

coma in my father on synthetic heroin

coma in the hands typing the insurance application

coma in the failed suicide attempts that succeeded

coma in the drunk cops brain damaging their sons

coma in the diabetic comas

        coma off the skyscraper.

i had a crush on Daria and Jane until i was 13,

i really liked combat boots on cute little feet, piercings, and witty femme folks with severe depression
         and perhaps BPD

suddenly real girls liked me and i thought it

wasn't such a sick, sad world after all
sorry, daria
      sorry, jane
       i'm a poseur

we make our first child and i throw it in the river like an oddly shaped rock
"there is no social home, no community

beautiful enough to put our child, to love it gently enough to be a child." i say.
we live in idaho for the rest of our lives and repeat this endlessly.
the river slams back and forth like a heartbeat.

id rather be Anthony Bourdain
        than God or Joe Rogan
noodles, meat, cigarettes,
                      whiskey & plane tickets

several oceans of things i want to know
and will eventually die from

she used to chain me at her feet and take the knife out, i could see it shine off my xany cheap beer eyes and i wanted so bad to be kinky and not be traumatized and in the ghosts of ptsd but then it wasn't hot anymore her shoes were still dirty my tongue was still clean,

my body is glass i am not able to worship a mirror.

i play death in my front yard.

what's the difference between a dragonfly and a gun?

the paramedics chase my dad into the house &
no one answers my question.

if you aren't too beautiful today,

  can you be clinically insane

                              with me?
you be the crack in the world,
mae,

and i'll steal you all the light i can grab.

the muralist is a noted womanizer & gives crabs to waitresses for a Saturday joke

he draws faces like he sees all of them and i believe that is the most horrible way to draw faces

i shot him in the throat with a bb gun & stole his paint supplies to vandalize government buildings

i am never going to be famous.

"*I do not think the libs are coming*," I say.

We laugh and put on the wolf masks again,

                       they don't filter the gas or eat the rubber bullets.

But we are still wolves.
Rip the neck.

it's wednesday morning

    and i'm the only one in the flowers.

they'll make me pay taxes for this someday.

the hole in my mouth got wider and you could see the little man inside.
he is close to dead and has a collection of little birds that I accidentally ate.
     i get indigestion and everything flies out at once. it looks like party streamers and the man cries out alone
and i swallow him whole.

we were too many kids to be loved like kids

 i hope we meet again as neurodivergent,
drugged adults
        with too much debt to smile.

the moment i smelled all those other drunks on your thighs,
i pushed you above the city lights

       and flicked my way into a gritty,
       disgusting beautiful place

like art but with acid reflux.

after my dad clicked his gun into the receiver,
the drugs got stronger
& the sex got weirder
& the shy executioner showed me her legs

& the mailman felt sorry for me and burned all the notices.

we ripped a mailman to shreds
                under the irrelevant moon

all of us dogs wait for the needle

we wag our tails and

kill until

we are the things that stand between the birds and the cats
it's a special way to be violent

to deny violence.

Lou Reed was a better poet than Keats,

Elliott Smith wrote bars that Whitman couldn't spit tell your english professor to piss off.

i don't want to go towards the light.

i almost wrote "you" instead of "i"

i will drink until the light is off.

if you hold me too close to the nervous system,
           i will shake all my blood
             onto the carpet.
you won't care about the roses,
      the carpet is ruined.

you'd prefer to die
    but you are a small child,
    stuck in a loop,
    as old as the world ever was.
    it's graves or
    it's guts.
    (you have no choice)

i am asked to tacitly
     scroll past
     1000s of
     injustices &
     deaths a day

     i will not be a war
     to you tonight.

the wolf at the door is   actually a very hairy neighbor
eating your mail

you can't pet him, he's feral

i don't trust
 anyone who stiffs servers
 or owns the Eagles' greatest hits.

come wet, i am hellishly
      drunk
      i'm everything
      this bar has tried to kill
      and
      i can show you
      how the dead push back.

*anyone who loves me or
         my poems* has a criminal
            record or wants one.

You built a
	dumb house
i tried to teach
	it calculus
but it ended up
	setting the cat
on fire it smells like
		weed and it will never
		be a skyscraper
i told it to
	be a church
	and it stole my
	wallet.

we like to drown, mae
it's a
joke to give up.
there is a long thin
line of bottles
pour the ocean
on the carpet
and get pissed at me.
i am leaving.

i used to make mix
    cds for girls they'd wrap
    their legs around my
    tired face.

i hid in there.
    i knew all the words.

everywhere in this hospital i am dying again
        there i'm in someone's bed lying on their horrified face.
    there i'm face first in the needle bin.
        there i'm trying to eat the HDMI cord to swallow FOX News.
    everywhere in this hospital i am dying
        and it's fun, i hope you know i'm having fun.

you said "let's just have the baby"
        and now you're knitting a
        noose, how small it is
        determines whether
        you're a killer or
        you're leaving me.

we reach out with
   the entirety of our
   pain and only
   our hands
   get there.

i don't have anything left to feed the wolves

so i split our kids up with
    a sad, knowing look

neither of them loved me enough.

            the rules were clear.

    you die for the ones that
    make you, not the other way around.

i carry a jar of your tiny flame into a forest
i wrap legs around it

i feel your skin
on the glass,
mae, this is where the fire starts, we rub sex parts like matches
& the planet becomes a star.

you're scared of a pussy

                        so you legislate the legs

the wettest you'll get

                is a nuke in the Pacific

the cat is in my lap it is
actually the light

I am with the cat

    I am not with anyone else
but the light,

But the cat.

It yelped & flew over the fence,
Mae.

I guess this would
be a good time to explain your mental illness.

*there is a faint
green that comes
off of me* at night,
swim by
my upstairs
window
i am no
comfort,
but
i am
here.

so i think we should wear the wolf masks to church
shatter the wine over the congregation
roll through the glass a
and drink our own blood
and his blood
like real drunken dogs & run for a hill,
the highest hill and die there sometime.

somewhere the lighthouse falls over.
we crane our necks and make candles out of the bugs

i don't think we're going to hell.

you do not know
who the little crow
 asked me to be
we eat wire together
 and talk about the way
 electricity has let us down.

don't drop your joy
> *on a man* or an
> ideal or the way
> you hold
> a partner on a
> suicide binge.

don't drop your joy
> on a joyless world

>> raise your head you
>> deserve your eyes.

all those other drunks were wrong,
not me

i'm true

i'm the high-functioning piece of shit that knows you best

they will cut a little thing out of you

you won't kick

you will love the knife.

if anarchists have a dress code,
you've taken mushrooms at the wrong party.

*i'm sick and i recognize
i have no history.*

the marigolds i stole from your dad's memorial
are wilting under my bed.

you are tired of all the weird shit i do.

drugs are everywhere in my blood.

i was way too little to be your father but that's okay dad i think we could have played more Nintendo together and I could have cradled your damaged brain like a stuffed animal I could have taken the things you put onto me and glued them into a school project and when child services took me away id show them the A+ I got and we'd still be a family, i would reverse you back to hope.

you are afraid now i'm gone

but we have different ideas of gone.

        the way you wake up alone
        is the way most wake up together.

*a mosquito lives
in your rib cage.*

this wild, useless,
frenetic violence.

i ask you to turn the tv off,
but its cries are too much.

we'll make a child in this bedroom
& you'll never forgive her.

*the moment i fingered the russian
perfume salesperson at macy's,*

she kicked me in the throat right before
orgasm &

                                                             then

i knew the cold war

we take a metro to the local grocery
like two people in love

(but one of us is)

        &

i don't even want you on credit.

i plant seventeen communists in my garden
and water them

      while i study Trotsky
in my boxers

No one reads books in my house &

I desperately want a garden
full of
human voices.

the workers have taken the
South Carolina penitentiary
& the guards are shot
like transmissions

        we line up traitors
                and throw them into
        thy te blood orange sun.

        revolt is the summer.

i had a nervous breakdown when I was 29 years old the pain under my breastbone was so everywhere that i smashed my head on the bathtub and ate my blood like tomato sauce it continued like this for 18 months 10 panic attacks a day dry heaving in subway station bathrooms leaving a fiancé and getting the worst case of shingles a doctor could recall i still fixate on the way that air conditioners function, the way I counted whirs to stay sane the curse of the generational brain, the curse of curses, the way we walk to the corners & hide until death rolls our number

*j'adore
your little cat*

we're sent in a Soviet rocket ship toward you.

we are your pets and we've got space helmets now.

                                        Meow?

                                      Meow!

we've got space helmets meow.

i barely slept on my grandma's floor for 11 months
she'd smuggle vodka into her church,

a cathedral of the bizarrely schizophrenic staining their own glass,

not with the blood or pinot noir of a savior
                                                         but of us.

it resolved to stab me before the construction workers woke up.

                                            it did not.

i'm sorry i got drunk and ghosted your birthday party

you will have to finger yourself tonight
and eat lots of cake

*i'm writing this poem for a
book*

it's not good enough to be in the book.

i folded it into a paper airplane
and lit it with a BBQ torch

i threw it at the neighbor child
the neighbor child is on fire.

i have a new poem

*mae, they don't understand how bored
of bodies* we all are.

the day you become a piece of light,

it will be a good day
full of love.

I kissed eight girls on my last day in town, none of
their tongues said anything inside me

one of them put their warmest thing in
my face, and i screamed down it like a hole

nothing is here.

here's the
    perfect love poem
ready
ok it goes like this
…
    …
shit i don't remember
…
    fuck…
ok
can we just forget about this?
there's a bar nearby

there are ten stray cats
    in my neighborhood &
at 3am they
    sit on my steps
    they are bored of
    my human form.
i am number eleven
they know it, we
will be brutal together
    i will kill the birds.
    i will live on your fence.
    i will die under a car.

i know a system that killed my friend

it lives a fat life
and calls my phone at regular business hours

"hello! I am a system that killed your friend
do you trust in me now?"

i'm not worried if god knows i'm gay,

        this guy gave me autism and whiskey, he knows i'm a kinky death trap.

        what ends the world, Lord, bombs or butt stuff?

today i woke up
> i made a really bad mistake
> mae,
> i've made a ton of really horrible mistakes.

*i hope when
they draw the blinds
on you,*

you're the kind of
dead you hoped to be.
i'm scared that
you left

but it makes
me beautiful
don't you think

i'm beautiful,
mae? blink

once for yes
in the
sky or dirt,
i miss you.

we're uncommon
       fireflies and our butts glow
       as we lock legs
       laughing. it's brilliant
       out here with
no clothes
       and your light

how do i tell the crow that
      i don't know where the dead
      animals live?
      it's hungry and my cat is still
      3 years from death.
      it doesn't care about him.
      it waits for my organs
      to give up from the whiskey.
      it's tired of my lies.
      it knows

i am

the animal
      it wants.

i will give you
>*the secret to a good fuck*
okay so there's this
other person and they might
have a hole, a hand, or a stick, or
some combo of this
or none of it (it's not important,
i promise)
and you should
probably listen to them and
love them for a fleeting second
even if you don't love them,
love them okay? and it'd
be nice to come
pretty hard, both of you.

i don't drink to get anything out of it
let humanity get everything.

it is too much anyways.

the only reason we have
mental hospitals
is because gardens
and graves
are too
close together.

it comes every so often
    at night,

        lights a
        cigarette, sits on
        my face

        puts it out on my chest.

        we live together like
        nothing ever happens

        i am in pain

my dad survived catapulting
    his head through a house,
      and a baseball bat to
    his soft spot

    he came home from the
    neurologist one day and
    said softly

    "i've got dain bramage"

    he walked up the stairs
    and i tell the joke
    to therapists now

when i found
     your nothing
i soft kissed
     your bellybutton and
     traced my fingers
          down the geometry
          of your legs
now i'd like my hand back
     or at least a place inside you.

the bowl is cashed & i've
        got an ativan dissolving
        under my tongue

        do you think the moon
fucks the ocean

 and that's
        why greenery explodes?

they took my grandmother
    away with half her
    intestines &
    my grandfather
    exploded his head upside
    down from a tree

    try to get her.

jesus died for my pedophilic bloodline

& a bunch of gated communities
       in the South and Northeast

                      mae, we do not crucify we
     sit poor & watch old Anthony
     Bourdain episodes w/ the
     needles on the bed stand.

i could not trust my body
       so i became a piece of
       light

       i startle the dogs
       to find you, mae

       "i'm okay," i say,
              "i'm just morning."

the thing i love about
>*bars* is that
>there's no good
>reason to be here.

>there are no good reasons at all.

this is how we move our
> *bodies so close*
> *together* that we cannot
> die that we cannot
> die alone.

i am this pigeon
 trapped in the station
 i shit on the rail
 i come for this bread
 i am a rat i am a rat i
 am a rat i am a rat
there is disease here
 and i am a rat

we like to build houses
    on people's heads
you laugh as they wobble
    and fall and all the babies
    inside crack on the ground
    like supermarket eggs.

we are dark and addicted
    and we put our pain in
front of everything else.

i love the way
           you love horror movies

and haven't murdered
           anyone yet.

*it is right there and you are not
        aware of it.*

       when you bury things

       when you scream

       when you hate

       when you pretend you're
       better than it

it is right there and i
    will not save
    you from it.

it was such a brutal night,
  i did not find you

Mae,
  do you hallucinate
into my arms or can
  i call you or
      put my fingers inside
  to get warm?

it is here in the mailman's suicide note

it's in the way you

took your daughter from herself it's in the headaches and the gun magazines and the comment sections and the drunks with their hellish crooked fingers and cocks

i am in love with no men,
only cats

the bird bobs down
the wire, my little
boy jumps for the fence & waits
& waits

the sun is a giant ball of death & fun &

he waits.

there is a nasty cut on my neck, mae,

                              it is the shape of your birth name

              i'd rather not say.

*i fell with
a woman mighty enough to own the spiders*

she

fucked my throat with her diamond peg & gouged this wandering
eye with a ruby stiletto.
it's not so far off from christ, Right?

(how do things like her die as things like me?)

[easy]

at 16 i was given the option

  to string a family back together

                or windex my father's brains off a motel 6 floor

this is the way i love so many loves.

i was supposed to be a priest & then i ate out my ex-girlfriend's mom at 15 &
jumped a suburb fence like a cracked out tigger
from her husband in ripped JNCOS.

do you know how sometimes a pedophile can make you a poet?

i am many poets.

the way you kicked off your shoes, mae,

i thought we
were the kinkiest, strangest ones in the Vans store

i do not believe in gods that don't worship you,

       and i do not care if the assistant manager kicks us out.

mae, i'm the space between the loves you'll throw away

everything will be very painful for 30 years

& i will be the cause of all of it.

i have not emptied a bottle as strong
as my spine
so i throw every one i can at it,

i black out so much in your arms.

*nothing hurts
enough*

i am about to
get off

and it doesn't
hurt enough.

don't hesitate to bleed out next to me, mae, i don't have band-aids but i have a glue stick and a really stupid idea

do you want to be a kindergarten art project or do you want to die?

i read a very bad poem that was very short.
it had 3.250 likes and I have a drinking problem.

i want to be
well but

I do not necessarily want
to be not sick…

if you like this poem,
well,
you're not really all that into poetry, are you?

In fact
you're shameful and tasteless & i think you're keen and very pretty.

the universe isn't a place,

it is in mae
it is a skittering heartbeat

when she is too anxious to come

i am just a moon look at me

you ask me to narc on my friends
and pay $13.45 for a banana

everywhere
the cameras

it sat hard on my chest at 5 years old
it stalked me to kindergarten, sat
at the tetherball pole, watched
my first kiss and left my first wife

i am in fits running from it, i have
no nervous system because of it

they will bury it on top of me,
                        assume i loved it.

i did not.

*the moment the panic
attack hits, i know*

i am an unceremonious
hole

that
follows
you
around.

there is cellophane
> *over the neighbor's flowers*
> and every brunch date
> with phones at the ready.

i am suffocating in a world
> that wants to be
> away from the world.

you are too manic
      to kill the pixie
    so dance and have
everyone misinterpret
      your murderous ways.

o

O

                                        o is a place

we don't live there we
just rent consciousness.

i of the moths i kill

the man who asks me for
coffee and smells
too bad to be human
in a Portland cafe

i who knows
i'm closer to him than
any of them

i of the moths i kill

if you stand between
two planets,

you will pull them together

                it will be dangerous,
                        mae, and you may kill

                            all the little
                            plants & aliens

but what if
you're a bridge
and not a bomb?

we had six-month old burrito wrappers
      under our asses
      and i never saw a Calvin
      Klein ad that looked
      or smelled like us.

i come awake under the robins
    that jump the squirrels

    everything feeds the tree,

even you and even me.

please bring back my
        childhood cat
his name is dusty and
        he has impeccable
        paw to eye coordination.
        i lost him when he died
        but things aren't supposed to die.

        so when you see him, he'll
        be alive because nothing dies
        i know it i just know it, nothing dies

some mornings a little
          piece of dream
          comes with me
i shush it & put it
in my bag, nobody
know it's here or
          how dangerous it
          is to be a dream.

he lived under her legs
	at the local bar,
	she'd
		get a bit tickled and rip at
the scruff of his neck
		when he talked i couldn't
hear him, he was like a horse
			without a horse suit
				i thought it was funny that
			he lived between this nice
			lady's fishnets but when he
			suffocated, nobody heard it.

*if the darkest thing you can think
of never comes true*

you will probably sell your art
just fine.

we chased the tech bro with
    m-80s in our hands

        i like when the fireworks mean something.

how many licks does it
   take to get to
   the center of you?

   you are actually a lollipop,

   this
   isn't about fucking

do not love
so more
   as to hold nothin
g
Else

&

do not love
so little
   as to fall alway
    s
Asleep

do not be a drug addict, mae

    if you're 5150d

    you will not be in rehab

you will be insane.

when you hold the little grey cat
you know that everything that can be crushed

                        will never be crushed.

not tonight, mae.

*war criminals don't just bomb they
also charge $75.000*

for preexisting
heart explosions.

(plead insanity

                                                                                     (get
                                                                                     free
                                                                                     foo
                                                                                     d

(then run

i will start sending you letters
as soon as the illness
gets worse.

they will be very short
and they will not help you.

*i used to shatter cds and
jab prettier faces into my face.*

after we'd lock lePps, 15, in your
mother's bedroom, you'd tongue
trace the dried blood on my cheek,
fingering yourself

fuck, if i know

i would open my legs but
you're too in love with the government

this milkshake is for the comrades, baby.

it is not

        a kind world, mae, but

    it has all this
    pressure in it

that can
                      explode
into
    radical love.

there are two of me
and like lovers
they touch briefly & don't know

Postscript

In the late 1970s, New York was a piss hole. However, it was a piss hole where artists could actually afford to fucking live.
Punk and hip hop were little babies. Cultures were elbow to elbow, running self expression like a current through the rotted guts of NYC infrastructure.
Landlords burned everything for the insurance grab. Anyone that wasn't pasty and affluent was redlined further and further into dilapidated areas. It's not far off from the bullshit of today, but is it ever?
Here is where Jean Michel Basquiat did a fuck ton of heroin and took the art world.
And it started with SAMO(c) -- a cryptic alter ego shared between Basquiat and fellow artist Al Diaz.
(Basquiat would end up stealing all the credit. He was kind of a dick.)
Unlike a lot of the graff writers most are accustomed to, this shit was stark. Black paint, clumsily sprayed, jagged mantras and directions for living. It was confrontational in that it took the space that vandals took illegally (air quotes) and took it somewhere else entirely:
"SAMO(c),,, AS AN ALTERNATIVE 2 "PLAYING ART" WITH THE 'RADICAL CHIC' SECTION OF DADDY'$ FUNDS,,,"
"SAMO(c),,, AS AN END TO THE 9 TO 5 "I WENT TO COLLEGE" "NOT 2-NITE HONEY",,,BLUZ',,,THINK,,,"
What the fuck?
What were they doing here?
If there's anything that reveals that "something else" in Basquiat's work, it's his understanding of space as a medium. Space, both its placement and its innate dominance over everything else.
When a writer gets up on a government-owned wall or sign, the text or image is inextricable from where it is placed. A pretty picture of a wiener is great on a trash can, but it's even better splayed across the front of an ICE headquarters.
Basquiat and Diaz went even further than this. They attempted to redefine, reconstruct the space they were touching. It was cryptic, self-important, often bloated. But it was fresh blood dripping from walls. It caught you in the gut if you were willing to dump yourself out of the space itself and into the narrative.

Basquiat continued this way into the art world. His best work challenged the space of a canvas to fight back. Tell me something different than what is true.
Here is where I think poetry can take notes.
The line breaks in this book are not pauses for breath. There are shapes and stops trying to communicate with the white space behind them.
I have taken several on the chin from about the content and presentation of my work. When I was a drunk, it made me insecure. Newly sober, it makes me enthused.
I do not claim to be a great like Basquiat. But I want to be a great. I am working and will work the rest of my life to be great.
We are not supposed to say that. We are not supposed to care so much about ourselves and what we are doing.
Fuck all that.
My life's goal is to imprint myself into the space around me. Kindness does that. Acceptance does that. Art can do that.
Not only do I want to live on in this space, I want to become inseparable from the space. I want to change the way the trees look. Or make loves feel more loved.
(Mae is a dream I always have.)
I am just trying to get up. The book is a sacred space. It is also something you can turn your nose up about as an author at a dinner party.
It is also bullshit. It is a space masking as a privilege. A book tells you what to do and where you should stick it.
I am just trying to get up. I want you to see my words where they don't belong.
Maybe you're fucking someone and a line pops in there.
Maybe you're telling your ex to eat shit and a phrase shows up.
Maybe you're about to die and it makes you laugh.
I am just trying to get up.

Made in the USA
Coppell, TX
19 February 2026

71716885R00083